MW01613788

JOHN PERIKOS

JOHN PERIKOS - Kallimassia, Chios 82100, Greece. Tel: 02710-20797, 51216. Mob: 094-5418907.

ISBN: 960 - 85009 - 9 - 0

By the same author:

1) THE CHIOS GUM MASTIC (in both English and Greek).

2) Translation into Greek of "A new theory Clarifying the identity of Christoforos Colombus, A Byzantine Prince from Chios, Greece", Ruth Durlacher - Wolper.

Theofilos photo was given by TYPOFFSET - Thessaloniki.

FRONT COVER PHOTO: Homère dèife dit aussi l' apothèose d' homere. Ingres Jean - Auguste - Dominique (1780 - 1867) Louvre.

"Photo RMN" Manager: Ph. Couton / C. Sanchez. Agence Photo: ATLAS 15815/N Client 30912 / Invoice N EP 220005.

The author and publisher of this book wishes to express his thanks to the following:

1. Brian Church, for his great help in preparing this edition.

2. Babis Koiliaris for his superb drawings.

3. Reunion des Musees Nationaux - Agence Photographique.

4. All the staff at the Museums, Libraries, Institutes, Organizations mentioned in the Acknowledgements.

5. All my friends and family for their great help.

JOHN PERIKOS was born in Kallimassia, Chios on 29.6.1954 and was educated at Chios High School. He then studied Naval Architecture and carried out postgraduate research in Management Studies (CNAA). After working for two shipping companies in Piraeus, he has worked as Sales Manager for the Chios Gum Mastic Growers Association since 1983. He is a member of the British Management Association, and an academic member of the International Committee of Christopher Columbus Quincentenary Foundation, Canada Ltd. He successfully prepared the submission bid to the European Union for P.D.O. (Protected Designation of Origin) certificates, covering Chios Gum Mastic, Mastic Oil, Chewing Gum ELMA, and Throuba olives. He has written many articles in Chian and Athenian newspapers. He was awarded an honorary Diploma by the Chios Homeric Academy for his research on Homer and a diploma by Christopher Columbus Quincentenary Foundation, Canada Ltd., for his research on Columbus. He is a member of BGS (British Graduates Society), EUROCLASSICA and HOMERIC ACADEMY OF CHIOS. He is the writer and publisher of The Chios Gum Mastic, Christoforos Colombos, Homer and Chios.

ACKNOWLEDGEMENTS

The author and publisher of this book wishes to express his thanks to the following:
1. ASHMOLEAN MUSEUM, OXFORD
2. THE BRITISH MUSEUM, LONDON
3. HERMITAGE MUSEUM, ST. PETERSBURG
4. KORAIS LIBRARY, CHIOS
5. TROIA - KUNST AUSSTELLUNGSHALLE DER BUNDESREEPUBLIK - BONN
6. MAURITSHUIS - THE HAGUE
7. BERLIN ARCHAEOLOGICAL MUSEUM
8. MUSEO ARCHEOLOGICO NAZIONALE, NAPOLI
9. KUNSTHISTORISCHES MUSEUM, WIEN
10. MUNICH ARCHAEOLOGICAL MUSEUM
11. MUNCHEN GLYPTOTHEK
12. ARCHAEOLOGICAL RECEIPTS FUND, ATHENS
13. METROPOLITAN MUSEUM OF ART
14. VATICAN MUSEUM
15. LOUVRE MUSEUM
16. HERZOG ANTON ULRICH MUSEUM
17. NORWEGIAN BROADCASTING CORPORATION
18. GERMAN ARCHAEOLOGICAL INSTITUTE, ATHENS
19. GOETHE INSTITUTE, ATHENS
20. DUTCH INSTITUTE, ATHENS
21. ITALIAN ARCHAEOLOGICAL SCHOOL, ATHENS
22. AUSTRIAN ARCHAEOLOGICAL INSTITUTE, ATHENS
23. BRITISH COUNCIL
24. GENNADIUS LIBRARY, ATHENS
25. HEINRICH SCHLIEMANN MUSEUM
26. MINISTERO PER I BENI ELE ATTIVITA CULTURALI - NAPOLI
27. HELLENIC POST OFFICE

CONTENTS
PROLOGUES

We are all the children of Homer. We have inherited his characteristics, such as clarity, anxiety, nostalgia, quietness and "blindness" - that mixture of fantasy and feeling.

His descendants, the Homeridae, made his poetry famous and spread it throughout Chios and the known ancient world. This was one of the reasons which made me write this book.

Another reason was that my research, which took about eleven years to complete, revealed less famous and some hitherto totally unknown documents.

Third, I've always wanted to write a book about this giant of a poet, in order that he be read and known by people all over the world. I have tried my best to shed light on Homer, hopefully pleasing and interesting the reader.

JOHN PERIKOS

THOUGHTS AND REFLECTIONS ON HOMER
AND HIS WORK

It's a rare privilege to come across a communicator who has the sensitivity of a young soul along with a wealth of life experiences and tragic adventures. Welcome to Homer. What's more, there's a general moral base on which the poet stands the ideological synthesis of his two great works.

Whoever hasn't tasted the milk of the knowledge from the "springs" of Homer over the years will have failed to taste the most basic delight that this milk offers: Timeless self-knowledge.

Though study of The Odyssey and The Iliad has neither a start nor an end, we do see the truth in the Platonic claim that Homer is the leader of all tragedies, in the full sense of that word.

In one work of literature, the moral conscience of the whole world is displayed, like a majestic overview of human life with thousands of new approaches and results. It is accepted that what we used to call the "Homeric Question" has ceased being a "problem" because tradition has already credited the two masterpieces to Homer. Most people today will agree that our task is to try to understand more deeply the technical structure and, of course, the art of our Iliad and Odyssey. The historical philosophy of the texts helped us to picture the conditions in which these epics were created although there was always a surrounding energy to be further examined and enjoyed.

The time has now come to tap that energy and to enter the magnificent inner rooms of the Homeric Palace where we had previously hesitated to set foot. To enjoy the riches and richness of this Palace which glitters like the Sun and lures us like the Moon. In the past, the critical brain and enquiring mind were our guides. Now, in this new adventure, we must rely on sensitivity and emotion. The voice of the ancient Rhapsodists of Ionia surely has something to contribute in these difficult times through which our world is passing. We shall find close to Homer the first value of the human soul. We shall find that we are not lost after all.

Our soul will become calm, and sweet, by reading Homer, stimulated through his verses, restored to order and given a thirst for justice and peace. The study of Homer helps us to refind the balance of our soul and to once again feel trust in man.

Professor **I. N. Avgoustis,**
PhD, History & Philosophy of Medicine,
PAMA Academy Member,
and Director of Pathology at Athens Medical Center

ANCIENT GREECE
THE GODS

The ancient Greeks with their clever and imaginative minds created a whole philosophical system which worked perfectly in the world in which they existed. This system interpreted all natural forces and unexplained phenomena that defined and ruled the Universe. Battles between Titans and the Giants ended with a generation of Gods in control. With these Gods, mankind made its first steps and, from the very beginning, paid the price for its weakness. Man's destiny was determined by the Gods. The twelve Gods of Olympus were created and shared all the virtues and many faults of mankind. They were magnificent, splendid, exhibiting genius, and had diverse individual characters. All became worshipped for many centuries afterwards.

The Gods had their own likes and dislikes for the mortal people and their behaviour was governed by this. In The Iliad Goddess Athena supported the Greeks, and Ares the Trojans. Very often the Gods used to leave Olympus and become mixed-up with human beings, sometimes to help them, but often to punish them and to control their destinies. The Gods also enjoyed "uniting" with the mortals, resulting in children who were called demigods (imitheoi). Gods used to eat ambrosia and drink nectar.

Zeus and Hera sitting on the throne. Winged Niki (Victory)
or Iris is standing in front of them.

The goddess Athina is depicted on a 5th Century B.C. jar,
with a shield on her chest, a helmet in her left hand and a spear
in the right hand (Vatican Museum).

THE HEROES

Mankind in ancient times experienced many difficult moments. The dangers of that troubled period included monsters, diseases and hideous creatures having human characteristics. Even worse, they were immortal by their divine nature.

Then the Gods decided to send to earth the Heroes. Most of these were demi-gods, born to a God and a mortal mother. The Heroes were protected by the Gods. Heroes were glorified for their feats and gained fame. Some of them did so well they became immortal.

Hercules: Holding the tripod from the Oracle at Delphi, the lion on his head,
his club and sword.
From Circa 5th Cent. B.C. (Martin von Wagner Museum, Universitat Wurzburg).
Photo: K. Oehrlein.

THE TROJAN WAR

The Trojan War was once considered to be a myth created by Homer's poetical imagination. But after the excavations by Schliemann and the discovery of Troy's ruins, this position was reconsidered. The Trojan War occurred in a period of great crisis in the Aegean world and was a cause of a series of uprisings that led to the overthrow of the Achaian-Mycenaean world. According to legend, the Trojan War began because the son of Priamos, Paris, kidnapped Helen, the daughter of Leda and Zeus (according to Tyndareo myth), and the wife of the Spartan king Menelaus. She was the most beautiful woman in the world. The Trojan War, which lasted for 10 years, was an extremely bloody one, with great losses on both sides. Among those who perished were the Greek heroes, Patroclos, Achilles and Protecilaus and, for the Trojans, Hector. This was the first known international war. It resulted in the free maritime passage of the Hellispont. It was the best ever Greek campaign (some 1,186 vessels took part) and, after victory, Greek domination of the sea was ensured and development of their maritime trade started.

The famous Wooden Horse - used by the Greeks to fool the Trojans - is seen here on a 6th Century B.C. jar. (Myconos Archaeological Museum)

A scene from the Trojan War. Achilles fights Hector (left)
while Menelaus and Paris clash (right).

Menelaus leads Helen out of a burning Troy.

PRE-HOMERIC POETRY

It is not known who the poets were before Homer, what were their poems and how they influenced Homeric poetry.

What is well known is that they were "planudians" (travelling poets or singers) who praised the adventures of heroes like the Argonauts, Agamemnon, Nestor, Patroclus and, the most famous of all, Achilles.

The singers used a lyre or a forminx. They would sing and dance lyrical songs or epic poems. The art of the singers was also a profession. They belonged to their own creative class, and were loved and honoured by both the people and kings.

Rhapsodists were the singers who came after Homer, from the 7th Century B.C. They sang Homeric epics and were given the name Homeridae.

A singer holding a lyre, accompanied by a dog.

THE ORIGIN OF GREEK POETRY & THE EPIC

From ancient times Greeks felt the magic, charm and power of the poetic word. The most ancient Greek poems took on a religious character, being hymns and appeals to the Gods and referred to the Gods' genealogy and their work.

During the time of the emigration of Greek races to the South, and when the first Greek colonies in Asia Minor started to be formed, poets began to reflect reality, what life was like at that time. Consequently, poetry changed character. Greeks were often involved in long wars, aimed at conquering other countries. From these battles, heroes arose, who were honoured and admired by the people.

Human values began to motivate people and were expressed in a poetical creation, a new kind of poetry which was the birth of the epic (epos). This specifically praised the adventures of the heroes. The old and new kind of poetry mixed together people as Gods, and Gods as people, all taking part in the heroism. The singers praised the acts of both people and Gods.

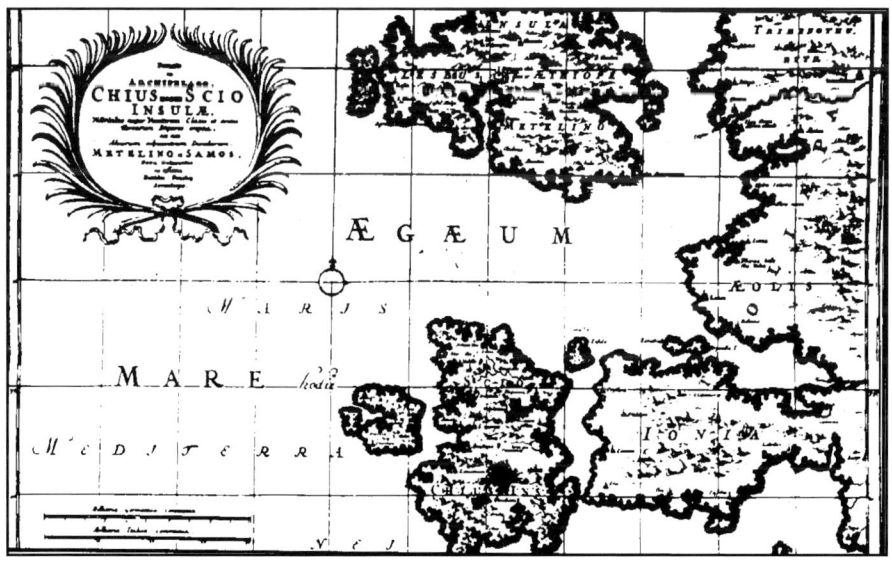

Map of Chios and Ionia, drawn by J. Bapt. Homans, 1690.

THE ACHAIAN CIVILIZATION

The Achaians were one of the stronger Greek races who came down from the North, at the same time, or later, than the Ions. They expelled the older inhabitants of Greece - the Pelasgians or pro-Greeks - and established strong kingdoms such as Sparta, Argos, Tirynth, Pylos and Mycene.

They made great expeditions abroad in order to conquer places rich in minerals along the coasts of Asia Minor and the islands. One such expedition was to conquer Troy Valley, which was likewise rich in minerals but, also, due to its geographical position, controlled the whole navigation of the Propontis and the Black Sea.

The Mycenaean civilization was developed from the Achaians. The German archaeologist Heinrich Schliemann (1822-1890), inspired by Homer, made excavations in Troy from 1870 onwards, which proved the existence of Troy's two cities, Ilion and Priamos, where the expedition and settlement of Achaians took place.

In ancient Mycene, Schliemann discovered in 1876 the royal tombs inside the Acropolis. The findings certified the power and grandeur of the golden city of Mycene, in full accordance with Homer's account.

Heinrich Schliemann on a Greek stamp in 1976.

(Photo: Hellenic Post Office, commemorating the 100th anniversary of his excavations at Ancient Mycene).

THE CONTINUATION OF MYCENAEAN CIVILIZATION

The Achaian dominance lasted from 1600 down to 1100 BC. When the Dorians started to emigrate to the South, they brought with them a markedly different life-style and customs. Using iron they enjoyed better armaments and destroyed the Achaian Kingdoms. Immigration occurred in the East and, in the Aegean islands. The Mycenaean civilization was continued through other Greek races like the Aeolians and Ions.

Mycene: Royal Tombs.
Section A of the wall at the ancient Mycene graveyard.
Photo: Hellenic Post Office, commemorating the 100th anniversary of Heinrich Schliemann's excavations at Ancient Mycene.

Sofia Schliemann, Heinrich Schliemann's Greek wife,
wearing Priamos' Treasure.

(Photo: Sofia Schliemann Papers, Gennadius Library, American School of Classical Studies).

Part of Priamos' Treasure, discovered by Heinrich Schliemann
(Photo by Peter Oszvald, Heinrich Schliemann Museum Ankershagen, Germany).

HOW THE HOMERIC EPICS WERE SAVED

The Homeric texts were made known in Athens by Ipparchos in the 6th Cent. B.C. (Plato, Ipparchos 228B) and classified by Peisistratos (Cicero, de Oratore III, 13t) and also by the philologists of Alexandria Museum. These texts were saved on many codeces from parchment (scrolls) of paper of the 10th or 11th Century. Some texts were in fragments from Rhapsodies and saved in papyri, scrolls and on many other materials during the Greek - Roman period.

Many codeces contain comments, such as those from the great philologists of Alexandria Museum, like Zenodotos from Ephesus (4th-3rd Cent. B.C.), Aristophanes from Byzantium (3rd-2nd Cent. B.C.) and Aristarchos from Samothraka (3rd-2nd Cent. B.C).

Apart from these comments, memorandums were also saved. These were written by philologists of the Ptolemian and Roman period. The Byzantine Lexicon of Archbishop of Salonica Eustaci (12th Cent. A.D.) consists of useful sources of comments for many ancient writers from Archilochos to Pindar and for many Latin writers too.

Thomas W. Allen, in his work (Homeri Opera), published in 1912, has gathered all known Homer's Works through codices worldwide.

ANCIENT GREEK TOMB EPIGRAMS

Homer is the virtues' preacher and hierophant of Gods,
the shining sun of Greece, and Muses' wonder,
the ageless mouth in the whole world.
The sea-soaked dust includes him oh stranger!

Antipatros of Sidon

Even if you strike with a hammer,
I will appear suddenly
like a Golden Homer, with Zeus' lightning.
Salamis is not my birthplace. Not Dimagoras
but Melitas will be my father.
Greece will not see this. You are looking for another poet.
Muses and Chios are my songs,
and will be taught to my Greek children.

Anonymous (probably Alkaios)

THE GEOGRAPHICAL KNOWLEDGE OF HOMER

The historian and geographer, Strabo, called Homer the leader of geographical knowledge, providing a wealth of reliable information. Homer clearly travelled in many countries for his poetry and the accuracy of his observations and geographical knowledge have been amply confirmed by archaeological findings.

Excavations in Mycene and Troy, for example, certify almost all of Homer's references. The clear descriptions of Ithaca and the island of Phaeaceans (today's Corfu), their history, the magnificent palace of Alkinoos as well as the naval experience of the islanders, show us what may be learned from Homer's own eyewitness.

Indisputable signs and many findings proved that Homer's city (Troy) was founded near the village of Issarlik, which is 12 stadia (over 2.3 kilometres) from the sea. The flow of famous rivers may have changed but we still see the ruins of Priamos in Troy, and the Trojan Valley and the channel of Hellispont ("Hellispont apeiron" - Endless Hellispont), which Homer so vividly describes.

The world at the time of Homer.

23

WHEN WAS HOMER BORN?

In spite of those who still argue over the birth of Homer, it is thought that Homer lived between the 9th and 8th Centuries B.C. It is generally considered that he was born a few generations after the occupation of Asia Minor by Ions. The Alexandrian philosophers say he was born 100 or 120 years after the fall of Troy (1184 B.C.).

Herodotus who lived from 484 to 425 B.C. considered that Homer was older than him by 400 years. But the Alexandrian philologists used to say that Homer was born 500 years before Herodotus. (With their calculations Homer was born in 984 B.C.) According to Oxford Marble Homer used to live in Volissos during the year 961 B.C. According to Vita Herodotea written by Pseudo - Herodotus, Homer was born one hundred sixty eight years after the Trojan War.

With Pseudo - Herodotus calculations the fall of Troy happened in 1270 B.C. and so Homer was born in 1102 B.C.

SEVEN CITIES STRIVE FOR HOMER'S BIRTH

Smyrna, Rhodes, Colophon, Salamis, Chios, Argos, Athens, or
Cyme, Smyrna, Chios, Colophon, Pylos, Argos, Athens

From the seven above cities mentioned in an ancient tomb epigram, five indirectly claim Homer. Only Smyrna and Chios make a clear and direct claim that the poet was born or lived there. In ancient times Smyrna was accepted as Homer's place of birth. Strabo and Plutarch called him Smyrnean. Homer's first name, Melisigenis, means that he was probably born near the Melis River in Smyrna. Also, ancient coins from Smyrna have Homer shown on one side.

According to Strabo, there was a sacred place called *Homerion* dedicated to Homer. Smyrna was built by Ions from Ephesus and then conquered by Aeolians from Cyme, and remained an Aeolian city up to 700 B.C. Then the Ions coming from Colophon reconquered the city. So if Homer was called by one historian "Aeolian", that means that Homer was born during the Aeolian occupation. The Athenians claim Homer indirectly, as Smyrna was a colony from Ephesus which was colonized for the Athenians by Androklos, son of Irodros. So Smyrna was considered to be an Athenian colony as the Peisistratos epigram says. It is also said that Homer travelled to many countries, came to Phokea and was hosted by Thestorides, in the New Wall near Cyme, where he performed his songs for a living. In Colophon and in Samos, where he was hosted by Kreofilos, according to legend one of his descendants gave Homer's songs to Lycourgos. From Samos he travelled to Athens but the vessel was grounded on the island of Ios where the poet fell ill, died and was buried there. Ios island claimed to have Homer's grave but excavations made there were fruitless. Only coins were found, depicting Homer. Chios is the strongest candidate to claim Homer, as a Head of an Old Man was found in Chios resembling Homer by J. K. Anderson during excavations made by the British School of Archaeology at Athens in 1952. Also, the Homeric Inscription of Chios engraved on quarry marble mentioned the number of vessels which took part in the Troy campaign.

A memorial to Homer in Smyrna.
(Photo: Homeric Editions, Chios, Prefecture, 1988)

Fimios died, he left his property to the child. After some time, Kritheida also died and Melisigenis succeeded Fimios in teaching. When he became alone, more and more people admired him, from locals to immigrants arriving in this place because Smyrni was a great port with considerable exports of wheat. When the immigrants finished their work, they began passing their time by listening to and watching Melisigenis.

ς'. Among them at that time was a boatswain from the island of Lefkada called Mentis. He came with his own ship to buy wheat. Mentis was educated, according to the education of that time, and knew many things. He persuaded Melisigenis to travel with him, to leave his teaching, and to receive from him a salary and have all his needs met. Mentis promised Homer that he would travel to kingdoms and republics well worth seeing, because he was young. It seems to me that with this decision Melisigenis succeeded. Maybe he was thinking of spending this time only on poetry. He left his teaching and travelled with Mentis. Whichever and whatever country Homer visited, he was watching everything and asking the people about local history. So it was easy from all of these trips to keep strong memories.

ζ'. At some time he returned from Tyrrhenia and Iberes, and reached Ithaca. Then it happened that Melisigenis' eyes began to suffer. Wishing to travel to Lefkada, Mentis left Homer in Ithaka with his loyal friend Men-

Homer travelled on Mentis' ship to many different countries.

28

toras, son of Alkimos from Ithaca, and asked him to take care of Homer, saying he would return to take him back. Mentoras took much care of the illness in Ithaca. He was rich and well-known among the Ithacians for his justness and hospitality. Here they told Melisigenis about Ulysses. Ithacians say that Homer lost his sight in Ithaca. I say that he recovered this time and became blind in Colophon. This is accepted by the Colophonians too!

η'. Mentis returned from Lefkada, stayed in Ithaca and took Melisigenis. For a long time he travelled with him. Coming to Colophon, Homer's eyes again suffered. He did not get well this time, going blind here. And so blindness returns from Colophon to Smyrni and Homer was given to poetry.

ιγ'. From this infliction, Melisigenis took the name Omiros (Homer). The Kymeans called the blind men Omirus.

ιη'. Coming to the town of Erythrea, Homer asked to travel to Chios. Someone who had seen Homer in Phokea greeted him. Homer then asked his help in finding a ship going to Chios.

κ'. Here in Chios the fishermen were doing their job. Homer, however, slept all night on the beach. When day broke, walking and wandering, he came to a village called Pitys.

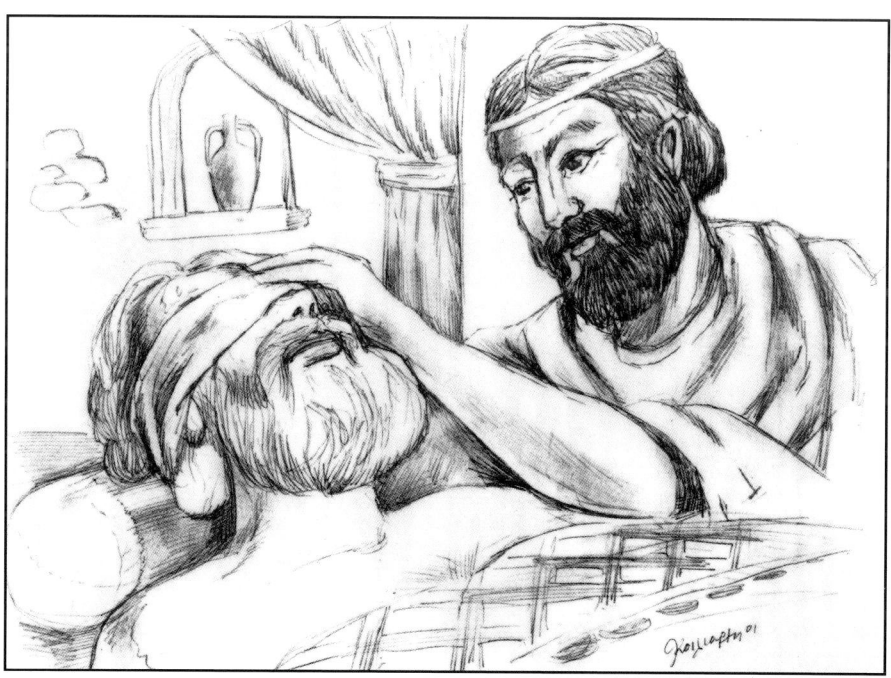

Homer again had problems with his eyes.

29

Note: *In Pitys village today, there remains a place with olive trees called Homerica or Teacher's olive trees. According to tradition, they belonged to Homer.*

κδ'. A servant Glafkos took him to his boss called Xios. In discussions with Homer, Xios found him very educated and experienced. Xios persuaded him to stay and become the teacher of his children. There in Volissos, Homer composed his "paegnia" - joyful works - such as Cercopes, Batrachomyomachiae (Battles of Frogs and Mice), Eptapaktiti and Epicichlides. He soon became very famous in the town of Chios for his poetry.

A servant, Glafkos, took Homer to his boss called Xios in Volissos village, where Homer stayed and composed most of his "paegnia" works.

κε'. After a time, he pleased the man Xios to show him the town of Chios, where he founded a school and taught the children his epics. The Chians understood that he was very able and many of them became his admirers. Homer became rich, married and had two daughters. One died unmarried, the other was married to a Chian.

κζ'. So from his poetry Homer became famous in Ionia - and all over Greece they spoke of him. Living in Chios, many people visited him, asking him to go on trips with them. He accepted, wishing very much to travel to other places.

λη'. All information about his birth, death and life, I have narrated up to now. Now, as regards the age of Homer, this anyone can correctly estimate. From the Ilion expedition, which was a result of an uprising by Agamemnon and Menelaos, one hundred and thirty years passed until Lesbos was colonized, because up to then it had no towns. After Lesbos' colonization, twenty years passed until Aeolic Kyme was colonized, today called Frikonida.

After Kyme, eighteen years passed until Smyrni was colonized by the Kymeans and in that time Homer was born. Since Homer was born, six hundred and twenty two years passed until Xerxes' passage from Hellispont. From this it is very easy for anyone to estimate the time, counting the Athenian governors. From the Trojan War, one hundred sixty eight years passed until Homer was born.

All the above are the basic points of Homer's life paraphrased from VITA HERODOTEA, written by Pseudo-Herodotus.

Notes:

1. Admitos: King of Ferae in Thessaly. His son Evmilos, was one of the heroes of the Trojan War. The Iliad B 714, 764, ψ 288, 354.

2. Homer took the name Melisi*genis* because he was *born* in the river Melis.

3. Fimios is a character in Homer's Odyssey. He is the famous singer who was singing in Ulysses' palace in Ithaca.

4. Mentis is a character in Homer's Odyssey. He is the governor of the island of Tafos.

5. It was important for Homer to reach Ithaca, the main location of The Odyssey, describing the island in detail.

6. Mentoras is a crucial Odyssey character, Book B 225, X 206.

7. Proclus' *Chrestomatheia* (a 17-20). The Kymeans called the blind men Omirus.

8. Pitys village today is called Pitios.

9. Eptapaktiki, we know nothing about.

10. Xios is the name of the man in Volissos, not to be confused with the name of Chios (Χίος) island.

11. Glafkos is the name of the shepherd who found Homer in Volissos.

12. Etythrae is the ancient town built on the foot of the mountain Mimas in Asia Minor.

13. On these calculations, Homer was born in 1102 B.C. (622+480=1102). Adding 168 (130+20+18) to this equals 1270 B.C. for a date of the Trojan War.

WAS HOMER A BLIND MAN?
(HOMER'S NAME)

HOMER'S NAME: The name Homer *(Homeros)* has many explanations. According to Proclus, Homer was given to Chians in captivity (as a hostage) from where he got the name Homer (Homer = Hostage). According to Pseudo-Herodotus, his first name was Melisigenis and he got the name Homer, because he was blind and couldn't see.

ΟΜΗΡΟΣ = Ο ΜΗ ΟΡΩΝ (The man who can't see).

According to Thomas W. Allen, Omaros was an Aeolic name, which could be found in the Pelasgians of Thessaly, who were the first colonists in Chios and Lesvos.

Homer, shown here blind from J. von Falke's book "Hellas and Rome", 1879.

HOMER'S BLINDNESS

According to historian Heraclides Pontikos, Homer travelled to the Thyrrenean Sea, Cephalonia and Ithaka and it is suggested that he lost his sight from an eye-disease. Herodotus concludes that Homer had been affected by such a disease in Ithaka and then went blind in Colophon. According to sources (i.e. various testimonies) it is possible this was "trachoma", an eye-disease present in Greece, including Chios, up to the late 1960s A.D. This disease was widespread in Egypt during the times of the Pharaohs. For these epidemiological reasons, we must accept that the "trachoma" of Egypt was experienced in Mediterranean areas around the 8th Cent. B.C. The majority of Homer's phraseology regarding his eye functions and perception of light leads us to the conclusion of Homer's personal experience of "Daltonism" or "Sensational Anomaly". Homer describes an amazing 39 different colours in his works, according to Spyros An. Magginas (ΕΙ ΟΜΗΡΟΣ ΤΥΦΛΟΣ) (1909). Sevasti Chaviara Karachaliou - a specialist in the history of medicine - believes that Homer's blindness was due to glaucoma.

*Professor John **N. Avgoustis** MD, PhD History & Philosophy of Medicine - General Pathology of Academy of Family Medicine (P.A.M.A.), Director of Pathology at Athens Medical Center.*

ANCIENT WRITERS ON HOMER

1. Aristotle (4th Cent. B.C.): In his work *Arts Rhetorica* (2,23). Alkidamas is quoted as saying: Homer was honoured in Chios, although he was not their citizen.

2. Plato (427-347 BC): Student of Socrates.

In his work *The Republic* (Politeia), Plato refers to Homer as the leader of all tragic writers and as the Greek Educator.

"Homer has educated Greece".

Aristotle

(Kunsthis-torisches Museum, Wien)

3. Lycourgos (8th Cent. B.C.): Lived at the same time as Homer.

Strabo wrote of Lycourgos "as some say when he met Homer, to live in Chios, he left for his country (Sparta) back again".

4. Thucydides (460-400 B.C.) considered Homer the poet of the Hymn to Apollo.

History, Book C, III 104.

"A blind man lives in rugged Chios".

5. Pindar. (522 or 518-422 B.C.).

Nemea VII. "I believe that the word (what was written) for Ulysses, stood above his sufferings, because of the affable Homer".

Istmia IV. "But Homer honoured him (Ajax) above all the people". Fragmanta incerti logi.

279 a. "Pindar said well that Homer was Chian and from Smyrni". Vit Hom Plut ii2 p. 244 Allen.

b. Homer...as regards his origin, according to Pindar, was from Smyrni. Vit.Hom.V2 p.247 Allen.

c. "Anaximenis so, and Damastis and Pindar the singer, they considered him Chian".

Thucydides

(Museo Archeologico Nazionale, Napoli)

HOMER, THE FORERUNNER TO HIPPOCRATES

When we refer to Greek medicine, the name of Hippocrates automatically comes to mind. To this day, doctors all over the world take the Hippocratic oath.

Some medical historians are so enthusiastic about Homer that they would like to name him as the most ancient Greek doctor. These historians believe that the poet Homer was a military surgeon with an excellent knowledge of anatomy. It's clear that Homer must have had some medical education, to judge by his medical descriptions, especially in The Iliad. This makes him the forerunner to Hippocrates.

The Homeric epics are full of medical detail, the first for ancient works of that period. Archaeological findings in many areas where a civilization has developed show that the legends and epics of the ancient Greeks were created on fragments of historical truth. Homer's medical education is indisputable.

In practice, every God of the ancient Greeks could bring any disease. Apollo and his sister Artemis were sent certain "arrows" that were used to do just this. Just as the Gods were helped by each other, so too the Homeric heroes came to each other's aid in order to survive such injuries and diseases.

(Extract from "The recognition of Homer, as a Doctor" by

I. N. Avgoustis and G. K. Kalantzis)

A wounded Patroclus is helped by his friend Achilles.
(Photo: Greek Mythology, Toubi's Editions).

THE ILIAD

THE ILIAD: The magnificent ancient Greek epic poem. According to tradition it was composed by Homer around the 8th Century B.C. With The Odyssey, they are the masterpieces of world poetry. The Iliad describes the Trojan War during its 10th and last year. Its duration is only 52 days. There are 24 Rhapsodies (books), with 15,693 hexameter dactylic verses.

The start of the poem is the anger of Achilles against Agamemnon. Achilles withdraws from the battle and the Achaeans are in danger of losing against the Trojans. Patroclus is killed by Hector, the son of Priamos, the King of Troy. Achilles, looking to revenge his friend's death, reconciles with Agamemnon, fights again and kills Hector.

The Gods take part in all the battles on varying sides. The King of the Gods, Zeus, is above all bias. He allows destiny to have its final say.

Achilles defeats Hector. Goddess Athena is on the left and Artemis on the right.
(From a 5th Cent. B.C. jar, Vatican Museum.)

BOOK 1

The wrath do thou sing, O goddess, of Peleus' son, Achilles, that baneful wrath which brought countless woes upon the Achaeans, and sent forth to Hades many valiant souls of warriors, and made themselves to be a spoil for dogs and all manner of birds; and thus the will of Zeus was being brought to fulfilment; - sing thou thereof from the time when at the first there parted in strife Atreus' son, king of men, and goodly Achilles.

Achilles, hero of The Iliad, earned the admiration of the ancient world for his physical strength.
(Photo: Vatican Museum).

THE ODYSSEY

THE ODYSSEY: This is the second greatest Greek epic poem, after The Iliad, which narrates the adventures of Ulysses after the Trojan War until he comes back to Ithaca. This epic has 12,210 hexameter dactylic verses. The main character is Ulysses. After the fall of Troy, together with his companion Ulysses starts out on his journey back to Ithaca.

Wandering around unknown countries, losing all his friends, he arrives via a shipwreck on the island of the Phaeaceans. He returns to Ithaca as a beggar, reveals his face to his son Telemachos and both of them kill the unwanted suitors of his wife Penelope. She recognizes her husband and the Goddess Athena intervenes in order to avoid the revenge of the suitors' relatives.

According to Zilbert Pillo, The Odyssey is a series of information signs for navigators, mainly for direction, that they must remember: the distance of travel between ports, the well-protected harbours, the sources of supply, etc.

Ulysses, tied to the mast, hears the Sirens' magic songs.

BOOK 1

Tell me, Muse, of the man of many devices, driven far astray after he had sacked the sacred citadel of Troy. Many were the men whose cities he saw and whose minds he learned, and many the woes he suffered in his heart upon the sea, seeking to win his own life and the return of his comrades. Yet even so he did not save his comrades, for all his desire, for through their own blind folly they perished - fools, who devoured the cattle of Helios Hyperion; whereupon he took from them the day of their returning. Of these things, goddess, daughter of Zeus, beginning where you will, tell us in our turn.

Muse in action.
(Photo: Theodoros X. Tsochalis, Homer's Iliad, 1992).

39

HOMERIC HYMNS

There are six major and twenty seven small hymns to ancient Gods that, from ancient times, are said to have been written by Homer. The main hymns are to Demeter the Goddess, Apollo, Hermes, Aphrodite, Zeus, Poseidon and Athena.

Frog-Mice Battle: Describes the war between frogs and mice. Consists of 303 verses and is an epic comedy. Zeus finally puts an end to their fight.

Margites: A derisive poem, referring to a fool called Margites.

Cycle: A series of poems (fragments) with events before and after The Iliad. From ancient times they were considered pre-Homer poems. The main poems are Titanomachia, Oedipodea, Thebais, Epigoni, Cypria, Aethiopis, Ilias parva, Iliu persis, Nosti, Telegonia.

HOMERIC LANGUAGE

The Homeric language consists of a majority of Ionic and a minority of Aeolic forms. Moreover, in this island (Chios) Homer was said to be born, and a guild who bore the name of his sons can be traced back as far as the 6th Century B.C. These coincidences are enough to allow us to say that Homer, like all early and unsophisticated poets, sang the language he spoke, and that that language was Chian. So we find that, as the ancients said, Homer was born in Chios and wrote in old Ionic. (Thomas W. Allen).

Archaeologists and researchers found that one third of the Mayan language was pure Greek from the Homeric period. Others believe that the name of America was given by the Indians who named the Europeans in America, Homerians. This was because they were speaking the Homeric language, and so they named the new world HOMERICA (AMERICA).

THE POETICAL ART OF HOMER

The first virtue of Homer's poetical art is the unity of the work, either in The Iliad or The Odyssey. From each work the poet took only one act from the heroes but this act was so intense and powerful that it kept the listener's attention to the end. Another characteristic is the paradoxical calmness of his work.

There are many nimble changes of narration from bloody war scenes to peaceful situations. Homer's poetry, though long, keep its harmonious symmetry. The poet uses the tonic dialect, having some points from the Aeolian, and the meter is relative to the magnificence of the praised heroes. The harmony of the language and melody of the lyrics are excellent. The poetry is expressed through politeness and depth of feeling. The moral of both the epics reflects the mirror of an advanced civilization.

THE HOMERIDAE

Thomas W. Allen writes that: "Antiquity presents us with a set of persons who bore the name of Homer in a patronymic form. *Prima facie* "Sons of Homer" should connect us with Homer, open an avenue to him.

The ancient world held the Homeridae for a family. Acusilaus, our oldest logographer, Hellanicus, older than Thucydides, said so.

The Chians laid claim to Homer on the evidence of this family resident in their island (Strabo 645, Certamen 13-15).

Further, the school - which is what the Homeric family amounted to - is a characteristic feature of the Greek mentality; the Hippocratean, the Platonic, and the Aristotelian have all left us their works, and under their masters' names.

Now when we find that Chios received a mixed Pelasgian and Euboean settlement, and remember that in Homer the "European Pelasgic" name applies only to the valley of the Spercheus, near to which it remained, Λάρισα Πελασγία (Pelasgian Larissa), may we not say that Homer or his father was a native of the Pelasgic argos, and even that on this account he chose Achilles for his hero?

The Homeridae, therefore, take us to Chios and to a Homer living there. But as to date all we can yet say is "earlier than Acusilaus", which means the sixth century".

According to Dimitris Siatopoulos, "Homeridae were not only singers and writers of the Homeric poetry, but also creators of the poetic literature themselves, having the style of the Homeric songs.

They had composing abilities, very strong memories, and survived the Homeric epics. It is certain that the Chian Homeridae were the leaders in saving nearly all of The Iliad and The Odyssey".

Ancient Greek references to Homeridae, noted by T.W. Allen:

1. Harpocration Ομηρίδαι (Homeridae). Isocrates' Helen (65)

Homeridae: a family in Chios

2. In general literature the Homeridae are occasionally noticed. Early in the Fifth Century Pindar (Nemea ii.1 sqq.) says: -
As the Homeridae
were singers and rhapsodists
most of the times they started their song
with praise to Zeus,
and this man (Timodimos)
dedicated his victory
in the sacred games in Nemea,
to the most-praised Zeus.

HOMER'S REFERENCES
IN THE ODYSSEY AND THE ILIAD

Homer's reference to Chios is direct in The Odyssey and indirect in The Iliad.

THE ODYSSEY: Book III, 168-172.

"And late upon our track came fair-haired Menelaus, and overtook us in Lesbos, as we were debating the long voyage, whether we should sail to sea-ward of rugged Chios, toward the isle of Psiria, keeping Chios itself on our left, or to landward of Chios past windy Mimas".

Menelaus and Nestor pass by Chios.

THE ILIAD: In Book XXIII 281-2 and XXIV 22, the sun rises from the sea and that means that the poet was seeing this sunrise, living on an island, and this was Chios.

"The morning planet told th' approach of light;

And fast behind, Aurora's warmer ray"

"The ruddy morning rises o' er the waves"

THE HOMERIC HYMN TO DELIAN APOLLO

If anyone from the mortal men
comes here (Delos) like a much-suffering stranger
and he will ask you:
"Oh maidens, who is living here, the sweetest of all singers,
and makes you so much more pleased?"
Then you all will reply honourably:
"The blind man who lives in rugged Chios
and to whom the epics, in the future, will reign supreme
against all other singers".

This traditional hymn is also referred to by Thucydides, History, Book C, verse 104, and proves Homer's great reputation.

Also in the same hymn, verse 38 refers to Chios as:

the richest and the most beautiful of the islands

The famous lions at the ancient religious and political center in Delos.

HOMER'S SCHOOL
References by Travellers and Writers

JOHANN MICHAEL WANSLEBEN (1673-1674) German Theologian and Traveller: "On the surface of the rock, which has been levelled technically, there is a round bench, about 2 feet in height, and in the middle a square stone of the same height with lions engraved on each side. These benches, as the locals say, were used by the students to sit on and to listen to their Teacher; the middle stone was used as his seat".

JOHN COVEL (1677) English Traveller:

"Here on a rock, called the School of Homer, can be seen an engraved bench with two lions on the sides and seats around.

DU PALAI (1696) French Naval Officer

"There is in Chios an engraved rock and very solid, which the locals call the Bench of Homer".

LOUIS CHEVALIER (1699) French Nobleman:

"The people of Chios call this place, School of Homer, and claim that at this place Homer taught to his students. They even show a place, which they claim to be the grave of Homer".

WILLIAM WITTMAN (1800) Doctor, Surgeon in the Royal Artillery:

"Under the rock, which I have described as Homer's School, flows a spring of water, which is famed for its purity and healing properties".

FRANCIS SACHEVERELL DARWIN (1809) English Doctor and Traveller, son of naturalist and poet Erasmus Darwin:

"This island was very interesting, because it was famous as the place of Harpians, and the School of Homer, which is far away, 2 hours from the town. This school consists of seats engraved on the rock, in a circle, having in the middle a stone, with four engraved lions, and because of this, they assumed that Homer was teaching there. On the seats there is a place for 40 students only, instead of one hundred".

KARL VON HAILBRONNER (1845) Writer and Traveller:

"I was going to see the most beautiful island of the Aegean Sea, this earthly paradise, where everything exhales Homer".

"There was a temple here, dedicated to holy Homer, and even now, stoned seats are around the stone".

VESTIGES D'UN TEMPLE DE CYBELE
vulgairement appellé l'ecole d'HOMERE.
A.P.D.R.

The temple of Homer's Stone.
Copperplate engraving 1782.
(Photo: From Konstantine Koutsikas' collection).

HOMER'S HOUSE

JOSEPH PITTON DE TOURNEFORT (1701) French botanist:

"Apart from Homer's School, the house where he was born, and where he wrote most of his works can be seen... It is easy for anyone to consider that this ruin (Homer's house) must have been in a bad condition, because Homer, according to OXFORD MARBLE (Marm. Oxon. Epoch. 30) lived there during the year 961 B.C.

The house lies in a place which has the poet's name, to the North of the Island, near Volissos, of which Thucydides, the writer of Homer's life, speaks the same name.

Volissos is lying in the center of the Ariusian valley, which was producing the nectar and maybe this drink contributed more than a little to increase the spirit of the genius Homer. On a coin from the collection of Cardinal Barberin, he is presented seated on a bench, holding a papyrus, on which there are some written lines. On the other face a Sphinx is presented, which was the symbol of Chios. Father Hardouin speaks about a similar coin. Mr. Baudelot has some similar coins from Smyrna, but with different description".

Homer's House in Volissos.

THE SO-CALLED HOMER'S SEPULCHRE
AT THE HERMITAGE MUSEUM

"Chios of ancient Iocc (Ios), in which during the previous expedition of Count A. ORLOBA - TECMEHCKAYO, a Russian Officer found an ancient Sarcophagus, the so-called Homer's Grave, which is now lying in our country at Saint Petersburg, in the garden of Count Straganova". Chapter II, p. 115. (Phillip Argenti's Book, Chios Bibliography, reference by Egor Metaksa, a Lieutenant-Captain, published in 1880).

"According to researcher Alexander Kruglov, this sarcophagus was in Stroganoff's possession and it was exposed in the garden of his dacha (countryside villa), then it was replaced to the inner yard of Stroganoff's palace in the centre of St. Petersburg, then, in 1930, to the Hermitage Museum. Several Russian publications discussed only the previous location of the sarcophagus in the garden of Stroganoff's dacha and mentioned that it was named as a tomb of Homer or a tomb of Achilles as well".

This monument represents Achilles dressed (disguised) in women's clothes at Scyros King Lycomedes' palace but he is discovered by Ulysses.

A photo of the so-called Homer's sepulchre at the Hermitage Museum.

THE HOMERIC EPICS AND THEIR INFLUENCE ON HELLENIC AND WESTERN CIVILIZATION

Homer's recognition in Greece started after the spread of The Iliad and The Odyssey. Around the 6th Century B.C., Homeric epics were being taught in schools, and young Greeks learning to read and write Homer's works.

During the 6th Century, at the Panathenea celebrations, Rhapsodists were singing both masterpieces.

Sculpture and later ceramic works were influenced by Homeric epics as indeed was the whole Greek world.

Alexander the Great thought that The Iliad was a war-like tool of virtue and used to place it under his pillow as a guide.

"The best poetry is that of Homer, and Homer is the best of the poets", said Hermogenis from Tarsus.

The Lyrics Alkman and Stessichoros owe much to the study of Homeric poems. Aeschyllus called his tragedies crumbs on the magnificent table of Homer. Sophocles imitated Homer's poetry so much he was called Filomiros (Friend of Homer).

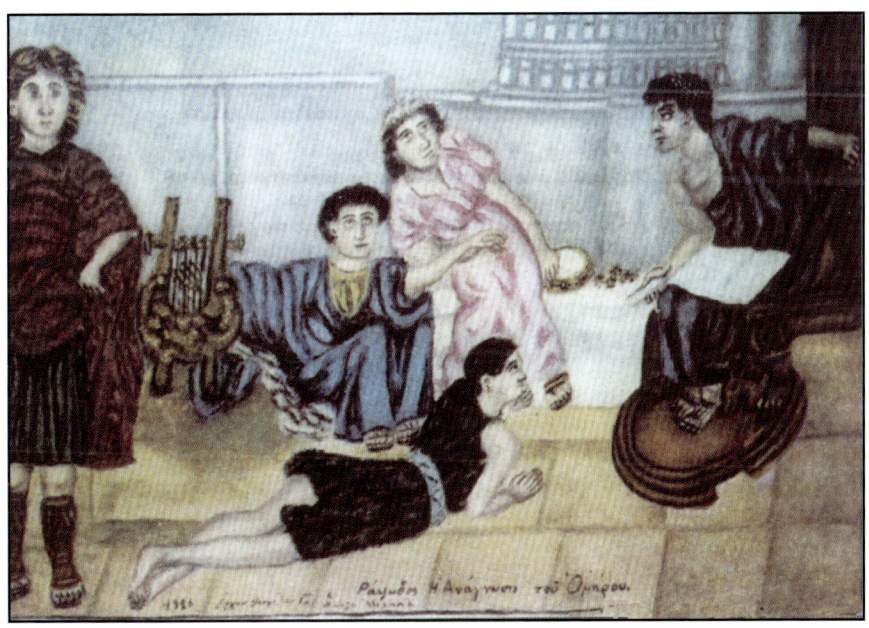

The Rhapsodist: Reading Homer.
By Greece's traditional painter, Theofilos Hatzimichael, 1926.
(Collection by A. Hatzidimos, Commercial Bank Edition, 1966).

53

In Rome the first poetical translation of The Odyssey was published during the 3rd Century B.C. The Iliad was translated later, during the rule of Augustus (1st Cent. B.C.). Homeric epics were then taught in Roman schools, and their influence had a great effect. Virgil was influenced by Homer, imitated him and transferred this affection to his students. Oratius worshipped Homer as the greatest of the poets and regarded him as the source of practical wisdom. Roman Generals Paul Aemilius and Skepion the younger also studied the poet's works.

Byzantines did not forget Homer, as the studies of Eustaci, Arcbishop of Salonica, during the 12th Cent. AD, certified.

From Byzantium, West Europe took the Homeric poems which, slowly-slowly, were becoming well known to a wider public.

During the Renaissance, Homer became well-known due to Latin translations. As the centuries passed, the Western world took a much greater interest in Homer's epics. In this way, Homer's thought clearly influenced Western culture.

The English poet Samuel Taylor Coleridge made an excellent translation of Homer's Hymn to Apollo. Lord Byron (Don. Juan. Canto, III LXXXVI) in his friendly and excellent verses for the Greek islands, and making an allusion to Homer, writes of "the Scian Muse".

The all-powerful British empire of the 19th century was mostly led by politicians schooled in the "Classics" at Oxford or Cambridge University. In the 20th Century and beyond, the richness and variety of Homer's works have been constantly recognised.

Alexander the Great.

54

HOMER AND POETRY

THE RETURN OF ULYSSES

I can see from here the roof of my house.
The first feeling of agony is going away
from the chimney, smoke's come out
My people are alive.
In the vessel my fellow seamen believed in that:
This could be true
Only the Moon remained unchanged here.

Bertolt Brecht (1898 - 1956)

RHAPSODY

God Homer, joy and glory of all the times
In my cold school days and in my education fulfilness
When I used to see my Teacher's ungracious fingers
Holding your big gracious book
I was waiting for this moment and you
Homer, used to come like a miracle.
My soul used to become like the clear sky
So wide and so crystal like the oceans' sapphire emerald.
The class used to become a palace with a throne
The school like a whole World, and
The teacher like a holy Prophet.

Kostis Palamas (1859 - 1943)

ITHAKA

As you're going to return to Ithaka
You must wish to have a long journey
Full of adventures, full of experiences
With mythical Lestrigones and Cyclops
Do not be afraid of the angered Poseidon
These kind of experiences are so rare to find
Your spirit must be high
Even if your full emotion touches
Your spirit and your body
You will not be able to meet mythical Lestrigones
Cyclops and angry Poseidon.
If you do not have them deeply in your soul
If your imagination cannot set them up
In front of you.

Konstantine P. Kavafis (1863 - 1933)

EPILOGUE

Homer wrote and sang his masterpieces and The Homeridae made them famous throughout the known world at that time.

Homer has been sung and read for the last two-and-a-half thousand years. In 4500 AD his great works will be just as famous, and just as relevant to human life.

The poet of eternity is still alive.

John Perikos

Homer's glorification.

57

COMMENTS ON JOHN PERIKOS'
HOMER AND CHIOS (1994)

The author of the Homeric Hymn to Homer, a work difficult to date but hardly later than the sixth century B.C., says that he is blind, and lives in rocky Chios (I.172). In ancient times, this hymn was believed to be the work of Homer; the great historian Thucydides was of this opinion. Other cities, notably Smyrna, also claimed him, but Chios had the strongest claim. Pindar and Simonides both said that Homer was a Chian. "By the fifth century", writes Mary Lefkowitz, The Lives of the Greek Poets, p. 151, «a reference to "the man of Chios" would be understood to mean Homer».

"It is this tradition about Homer, which is still very much alive among the people of the island, that has provided Mr. Perikos with the subject of his fascinating book."

"The reader of his book is listening to a Greek voice, which brings him into contact with the traditions of a rich popular culture, and he will be heartily grateful to the author to whom he owes this privilege".

SIR HUGH LLOYD-JONES
Formerly Regius Professor of Greek
University of Oxford

"In the Spring of 1952 the British School at Athens carried out the first of what was to prove a highly successful series of excavations on the island of Chios".

"A head was found in which, with no great stretch of the imagination, one may recognize the "blind old man dwelling in rocky Chios" who stands at the very beginning of Western thought".

"Mr. Perikos has here collected the many ancient testimonies to the connections between Chios and Homer. His work will be of value to all visitors to the island, whether or not they profess themselves Homeric scholars".

J. K. ANDERSON
Professor of Classical Archaeology
University of California at Berkeley

BIBLIOGRAPHY

1. Homer's Odyssey, selections from the D - Class High School - Nik. Eleopoulou, Kalleroï Eleopoulou, Athens 1969.

2. Homer's Iliad - Patakis Editions Vol.A p.3, S. Patakis - A. Batzoglou.

3. Homeros - Pavlos Drandakis - Athens 1933.

4. Archaeology of Chios - G. Chrysseidou - 1820.

5. The Archaeology and Early History of Chios - Eleftherios Yalouris - Oct. 1976 - Oxford University. Thesis submitted for D. Phil. Degree.

6. Ancient Greece at Work - An Economic History of Greece, From the Homeric Period to the Roman Conquest - Gustave Glotz, Routledge & Kegan Paul Ltd - London 1926.

7. Soviet Encyclopaedia Vols. 14 & 25.

8. Homeric Editions (1539 - 1955) Chios Prefecture. Korais Library of Chios 1988.

9. Gilbert Pillo. The secret code of Odyssey. Greeks in the Atlantic Ocean. Smyrniotakis Edition p. 159.

10. Chios from Geographers and Travellers. P. Argenti - S. Kyriakidis. Vol A, B, C. Estia 1946.

11. Chiaki - G. Dermitzakis - Prof. of Geology at Athens University.

12. Chios - National Bank of Greece publication 1974.

13. National Geography, December 1987.

14. Chios calendar 1976, Pseudo - Herodotus: HOMER'S LIFE - Chaviara Editions.

15. I. Th. Kakrides - History of the Greek Nation Vol. B p. 158.

16. K. Amantos - About Homer traditions in Chios - Istros 1936.

17. Filipou L. Chryssoveloni - Chios and Chians through the centuries, Athens 1938.

18. Katherine Esdaile - An Essay Towards the Classification of Homeric Coin Types (The Journal of Hellenic Studies. Volume XXXII (1912). M. DCCCC.XII.

19. The Arundel Marbles - D.E.L Haynes - OXFORD, University of Oxford - Ashmolean Museum.

20. Pindari Carmina - CVM Fragments - C.M. Bowra - Collegi Wadhami

Socivs Oxon II e Typographeo Clarendoniano.

21. Allen, Thomas W. The Origins and Transmissions - Oxford at the Clarendon Press 1924. 8.

22. Dimitri Siatopoulos. Homer and Homeridae - Chios in the center of the Homeric matter.

23. Chios Bibliography. Philip Argenti, with a Preface by Professor J. L. Myres - Oxford at the Clarendon Press 1940.

24. Spyros Kateras - Publisher and Historian, Manchester, N. H. 1937 USA. "Christofer Columbus was a Greek and his real name was Nikolaos Ypshilantis, from the Greek island Chios".

25. J. Irving Manatt - Prof. of Greek in Brown University, sometime American Consul at Athens - Aegean Days - London, John Murray Albemarble str. 1913.

26. The Ancient Greek Epigrams - Vas. I. Lazanas - Tsapetas Editions, Athens 1989.

27. HOMERI OPERA - Thomas W. Allen - OXON II - Great Britain.

28. Alexander Pope Esq. The Iliad of Homer - London. Published by T. Albman, 24 Holborn Hill. (March 25, 1720).

29. Thucydides - Libri I-IV-OXON II 1900 - Great Britain - History C III 104.

30. Homer and Odysseus - Spiros Dendrinos - Athens 1991.

31. Triantafyllos Dellis - The Iliad of Homer - Gutenberg - 1979.

32. The History of the Hellenic Nation - Ekdotiki Athenon A.E. 1971. Volume B - Archaic Hellenism.

33. Encyclopaedia Hydria. Vol. 42/51.

34. Greek Mythology - Toubi's Editions - Sofia Souli.

35. HOMER, THE ILIAD, A.T. MURRAY, Ph.D. I, Cambridge Massachusetts, Harvard University Press, London, William Heinemann Ltd, MCMLXXXVIII The Loeb Classical Library. (See The Iliad Book 1).

36. HOMER, THE ODYSSEY Books 1-12 A. T. MURRAY, Revised by George E. Dimock Harvard University Press, Cambridge Massachusetts, London, England 1995. (See The Odyssey Book 1).

37. The recognition of Homer as a Doctor.

I. N. Avgoustis - Professor of History & Philosophy of Medicine, G. K. Kalantzis - History of Medicine, Athens University Medical School.